MW00737515

for

_____ Dad _____

from

_____ Jordan _____

*The integrity of the upright
guides them.*

—Proverbs 11:3 (NIV)

Authentic Publishing
We welcome your questions and comments.

USA	1820 Jet Stream Drive, Colorado Springs, CO 80921
	www.authenticbooks.com
UK	9 Holdom Avenue, Bletchley, Milton Keynes, Bucks, MK1
	1QR
	www.authenticmedia.co.uk
India	Logos Bhavan, Medchal Road, Jeedimetla Village,
	Secunderabad
	500 055, A.P.

God's Promises on Character
ISBN 978-1-934068-90-8

A catalog record for this book is available from the Library of Congress.

13 12 11 10 09 08 / 1 2 3 4 5 6

Printed in the United States of America

GOD'S PROMISES

on Character

GOD'S PROMISES   D'S PRO

CONTENTS

ATTRIBUTES OF DISTINCTIVE

Character

*People who love your teachings
will find true peace. Nothing can
make those people fall.*

—Psalm 119:165 (ERV)

A Love FOR PEACE

The work of righteousness will be peace, and the effect of righteousness, quietness and assurance forever.
—*Isaiah 32:17 (NKJV)*

Consider the blameless, observe the upright; there is a future for the man of peace.
—*Psalm 37:37 (NIV)*

You will keep in perfect peace all who trust in you, all whose thoughts are fixed on you!
—*Isaiah 26:3 (NLT)*

Therefore let us pursue the things which make for peace and the things by which one may edify another.
—*Romans 14:19 (NKJV)*

Try to live in peace with all people.
And try to live lives free from sin. If a
person's life is not holy, then he will
never see the Lord.
—*Hebrews 12:14 (ERV)*

I will listen to what God the LORD will
say; he promises peace to his people,
his saints—but let them not return to
folly.
—*Psalm 85:8 (NIV)*

A sound heart is life to the body, but
envy is rottenness to the bones.
—*Proverbs 14:30 (NKJV)*

Salt is good for seasoning. But if it
loses its flavor, how do you make
it salty again? You must have the
qualities of salt among yourselves and
live in peace with each other.
—*Mark 9:50 (NLT)*

Whatever you have learned or received or heard from me, or seen in me—put it into practice. And the God of peace will be with you.

—*Philippians 4:9 (NIV)*

I leave you peace. It is my own peace I give you. I give you peace in a different way than the world does. So don't be troubled. Don't be afraid.

—*John 14:27 (ERV)*

When a man's ways please the LORD, He makes even his enemies to be at peace with him.

—*Proverbs 16:7 (NKJV)*

Those who walk uprightly enter into peace; they find rest as they lie in death.

—*Isaiah 57:2 (NIV)*

Run from anything that stimulates youthful lusts. Instead, pursue righteous living, faithfulness, love, and peace. Enjoy the companionship of those who call on the Lord with pure hearts.
　　　—2 Timothy 2:22 (NLT)

He who would love life and see good days, let him refrain his tongue from evil, and his lips from speaking deceit. Let him turn away from evil and do good; let him seek peace and pursue it.
　　　—1 Peter 3:10–11 (NKJV)

Depart from evil and do good; seek peace and pursue it.
　　　—Psalm 34:14 (NKJV)

Do the best you can to live in peace with all people.
　　　—Romans 12:18 (ERV)

But the wisdom from above is first of all pure. It is also peace loving, gentle at all times, and willing to yield to others. It is full of mercy and good deeds. It shows no favoritism and is always sincere. And those who are peacemakers will plant seeds of peace and reap a harvest of righteousness.

—*James 3:17–18 (NLT)*

But you will have a son who will be a man of peace and rest, and I will give him rest from all his enemies on every side. His name will be Solomon, and I will grant Israel peace and quiet during his reign. He is the one who will build a house for my Name. He will be my son, and I will be his father. And I will establish the throne of his kingdom over Israel forever.

—*1 Chronicles 22:9–10 (NIV)*

CHARACTER PORTRAIT
ABRAHAM BARGAINS FOR *Peace*

So Abram went up from Egypt to the
Negev, with his wife and everything he
had, and Lot went with him. Abram had
become very wealthy in livestock and in
silver and gold.

From the Negev he went from place
to place until he came to Bethel, to the
place between Bethel and Ai where his
tent had been earlier and where he had
first built an altar. There Abram called
on the name of the LORD.

Now Lot, who was moving about with
Abram, also had flocks and herds and
tents. But the land could not support
them while they stayed together, for
their possessions were so great that
they were not able to stay together.
And quarreling arose between Abram's
herdsmen and the herdsmen of Lot.
The Canaanites and Perizzites were also

living in the land at that time.

So Abram said to Lot, "Let's not have any quarreling between you and me, or between your herdsmen and mine, for we are brothers. Is not the whole land before you? Let's part company. If you go to the left, I'll go to the right; if you go to the right, I'll go to the left."

Lot looked up and saw that the whole plain of the Jordan was well watered, like the garden of the LORD, like the land of Egypt, toward Zoar. (This was before the LORD destroyed Sodom and Gomorrah.) So Lot chose for himself the whole plain of the Jordan and set out toward the east. The two men parted company: Abram lived in the land of Canaan, while Lot lived among the cities of the plain and pitched his tents near Sodom. Now the men of Sodom were wicked and were sinning greatly against the LORD.

—*Genesis 13:1–13 (NIV)*

And the LORD said, "Because the outcry against Sodom and Gomorrah is great, and because their sin is very grave, I will go down now and see whether they have done altogether according to the outcry against it that has come to Me; and if not, I will know."

Then the men turned away from there and went toward Sodom, but Abraham still stood before the LORD. And Abraham came near and said, "Would You also destroy the righteous with the wicked? Suppose there were fifty righteous within the city; would You also destroy the place and not spare it for the fifty righteous that were in it?" . . .

So the LORD said, "If I find in Sodom fifty righteous within the city, then I will spare all the place for their sakes."

Then Abraham answered and said, "Indeed now, I who am but dust and ashes have taken it upon myself to speak to the Lord: Suppose there were five less than the fifty righteous; would You destroy all of the city for lack of five?"

So He said, "If I find there forty-five, I will not destroy it."

And he spoke to Him yet again and said, "Suppose there should be forty found there?"

So He said, "I will not do it for the sake of forty."

Then he said, "Let not the Lord be angry, and I will speak: Suppose thirty should be found there?"

So He said, "I will not do it if I find thirty there."

And he said, "Indeed now, I have taken it upon myself to speak to the Lord: Suppose twenty should be found there?"

So He said, "I will not destroy it for the sake of twenty."

Then he said, "Let not the Lord be angry, and I will speak but once more: Suppose ten should be found there?"

And He said, "I will not destroy it for the sake of ten." So the LORD went His way as soon as He had finished speaking with Abraham; and Abraham returned to his place.

—*Genesis 18:20–24, 26–33
(NKJV)*

And not only that, but we also glory in tribulations, knowing that tribulation produces perseverance; and perseverance, character; and character, hope.

> —*Romans 5:3–4 (NKJV)*

Therefore, since we are surrounded by such a huge crowd of witnesses to the life of faith, let us strip off every weight that slows us down, especially the sin that so easily trips us up. And let us run with endurance the race God has set before us.

> —*Hebrews 12:1 (NLT)*

Your promise revives me; it comforts me in all my troubles.

> —*Psalm 119:50 (NLT)*

Blessed is the man who perseveres under trial, because when he has stood the test, he will receive the crown of life that God has promised to those who love him.

—*James 1:12 (NIV)*

Brothers and sisters, follow the example of the prophets who spoke for the Lord (God). They suffered many bad things, but they were patient. We say that those people who accepted their troubles with patience are now happy. You have heard about Job's patience. You know that after all Job's trouble, the Lord helped him. This shows that the Lord is full of mercy and is kind.

—*James 5:10–11 (ERV)*

Consider my affliction and deliver me, for I do not forget Your law.

—*Psalm 119:153 (NKJV)*

For this reason I also suffer these things; nevertheless I am not ashamed, for I know whom I have believed and am persuaded that He is able to keep what I have committed to Him until that Day.

—*2 Timothy 1:12 (NKJV)*

And you became like us and like the Lord. You suffered much, but still you accepted the teaching with joy. The Holy Spirit gave you that joy.

—*1 Thessalonians 1:6 (ERV)*

So accept sufferings like those sufferings are a father's punishment. God does these things to you like a father punishing his children. All children are punished by their fathers.

—*Hebrews 12:7 (ERV)*

But he said to me, "My grace is sufficient for you, for my power is made perfect in weakness." Therefore I will boast all the more gladly about my weaknesses, so that Christ's power may rest on me. That is why, for Christ's sake, I delight in weaknesses, in insults, in hardships, in persecutions, in difficulties. For when I am weak, then I am strong.
     —2 Corinthians 12:9–10 (NIV)

My health may fail, and my spirit may grow weak, but God remains the strength of my heart; he is mine forever.
     —Psalm 73:26 (NLT)

He will call upon me, and I will answer him; I will be with him in trouble, I will deliver him and honor him.
     —Psalm 91:15 (NIV)

Can anything ever separate us from Christ's love? Does it mean he no longer loves us if we have trouble or calamity, or are persecuted, or hungry, or destitute, or in danger, or threatened with death? . . . No, despite all these things, overwhelming victory is ours through Christ, who loved us.

And I am convinced that nothing can ever separate us from God's love. Neither death nor life, neither angels nor demons, neither our fears for today nor our worries about tomorrow—not even the powers of hell can separate us from God's love. No power in the sky above or in the earth below—indeed, nothing in all creation will ever be able to separate us from the love of God that is revealed in Christ Jesus our Lord.

—Romans 8:35, 37–39 (NLT)

The Lord is my strength. He saves me, and I sing songs of praise to him. The Lord is my God, and I praise him. The Lord is the God of my ancestors, and I honor him.
　　—*Exodus 15:2 (ERV)*

Not only so, but we also rejoice in our sufferings, because we know that suffering produces perseverance.
　　—*Romans 5:3 (NIV)*

You therefore must endure hardship as a good soldier of Jesus Christ.
　　—*2 Timothy 2:3 (NKJV)*

So do not throw away this confident trust in the Lord. Remember the great reward it brings you! Patient endurance is what you need now, so that you will continue to do God's will. Then you will receive all that he has promised.
　　—*Hebrews 10:35–36 (NLT)*

Figs might not grow on the fig trees. Grapes might not grow on the vines. Olives might not grow on the olive trees. Food might not grow in the fields. There might not be any sheep in the pens. There might not be any cattle in the barns. But I will still be glad in the Lord. I will rejoice in God my savior. The Lord, my Master, gives me my strength. He helps me run fast like a deer. He leads me safely on the mountains.

—*Habakkuk 3:17–19 (ERV)*

Now may the Lord direct your hearts into the love of God and into the patience of Christ.

—*2 Thessalonians 3:5 (NKJV)*

CHARACTER PORTRAIT

By faith Jacob, when he was dying, blessed each of the sons of Joseph, and worshiped, leaning on the top of his staff.

By faith Joseph, when he was dying, made mention of the departure of the children of Israel, and gave instructions concerning his bones. . . .

By faith Moses, when he became of age, refused to be called the son of Pharaoh's daughter, choosing rather to suffer affliction with the people of God than to enjoy the passing pleasures of sin, esteeming the reproach of Christ greater riches than the treasures in Egypt; for he looked to the reward.

By faith he forsook Egypt, not fearing the wrath of the king; for he endured as seeing Him who is invisible. By faith he kept the Passover and the sprinkling of blood, lest he who destroyed the firstborn should touch them.

By faith they passed through the Red Sea as by dry land, whereas the Egyptians, attempting to do so, were drowned.

By faith the walls of Jericho fell down after they were encircled for seven days. By faith the harlot Rahab did not perish with those who did not believe, when she had received the spies with peace.

And what more shall I say? For the time would fail me to tell of Gideon and Barak and Samson and Jephthah, also of David and Samuel and the prophets: who through faith subdued kingdoms, worked righteousness, obtained promises, stopped the mouths of lions, quenched the violence of fire, escaped the edge of the sword, out of weakness were made strong, became valiant in battle, turned to flight the armies of the aliens. Women received their dead raised to life again.

Others were tortured, not accepting deliverance, that they might obtain a better resurrection. Still others had trial of mockings and scourgings, yes, and of chains and imprisonment. They were stoned, they were sawn in two, were tempted, were slain with the sword. They wandered about in sheepskins and goatskins, being destitute, afflicted, tormented—of whom the world was not worthy. They wandered in deserts and mountains, in dens and caves of the earth.

And all these, having obtained a good testimony through faith, did not receive the promise.

—*Hebrews 11:21–22, 24–39*
(NKJV)

Actions THAT HONOR GOD

If you are wise and understand God's ways, prove it by living an honorable life, doing good works with the humility that comes from wisdom.
>   —*James 3:13 (NLT)*

My children, our love should not be only words and talk. No! Our love must be true love. We should show our love by the things we do.
>   —*1 John 3:18 (ERV)*

Do not be deceived: "Evil company corrupts good habits."
>   —*1 Corinthians 15:33 (NKJV)*

May integrity and uprightness protect me, because my hope is in you.
>   —*Psalm 25:21 (NIV)*

Don't continue bragging! Don't speak proud words! Why? Because the Lord God knows everything, God leads and judges people.

—*1 Samuel 2:3 (ERV)*

I have followed your commands, which keep me from following cruel and evil people.

—*Psalm 17:4 (NLT)*

Let integrity and uprightness preserve me, for I wait for You.

—*Psalm 25:21 (NKJV)*

A person might say, "You have faith, but I do things. Show me your faith! Your faith does nothing. I will show you my faith by the things I do."

—*James 2:18 (ERV)*

Lord, try me and test me. Look closely
into my heart and mind. I always see
your tender love. I live by your truths.
        —*Psalm 26:2–3 (ERV)*

And let us consider how we may spur
one another on toward love and good
deeds.
        —*Hebrews 10:24 (NIV)*

For you know that you ought to imitate
us. We were not idle when we were
with you. We never accepted food
from anyone without paying for it.
We worked hard day and night so we
would not be a burden to any of you.
We certainly had the right to ask you to
feed us, but we wanted to give you an
example to follow.
        —*2 Thessalonians 3:7–9 (NLT)*

Command those who are rich in this present age not to be haughty, nor to trust in uncertain riches but in the living God, who gives us richly all things to enjoy. Let them do good, that they be rich in good works, ready to give, willing to share.
　　　—*1 Timothy 6:17–18 (NKJV)*

Then the LORD said to Satan, "Have you considered My servant Job, that there is none like him on the earth, a blameless and upright man, one who fears God and shuns evil? And still he holds fast to his integrity, although you incited Me against him, to destroy him without cause."
　　　—*Job 2:3 (NKJV)*

But if you remain in me and my
words remain in you, you may ask
for anything you want, and it will be
granted!

—*John 15:7 (NLT)*

Righteousness guards the man of
integrity, but wickedness overthrows
the sinner.

—*Proverbs 13:6 (NIV)*

A good, honest person is safe. But
a crooked person who cheats will be
caught.

—*Proverbs 10:9 (ERV)*

CHARACTER PORTRAIT
NOAD DID WHAT WAS *Right*

The LORD saw how great man's wickedness on the earth had become, and that every inclination of the thoughts of his heart was only evil all the time. The LORD was grieved that he had made man on the earth, and his heart was filled with pain. So the LORD said, "I will wipe mankind, whom I have created, from the face of the earth—men and animals, and creatures that move along the ground, and birds of the air—for I am grieved that I have made them." But Noah found favor in the eyes of the LORD.

This is the account of Noah.

Noah was a righteous man, blameless among the people of his time, and he walked with God. Noah had three sons:

Shem, Ham and Japheth.

Now the earth was corrupt in God's sight and was full of violence. God saw how corrupt the earth had become, for all the people on earth had corrupted their ways. So God said to Noah, "I am going to put an end to all people, for the earth is filled with violence because of them. I am surely going to destroy both them and the earth. So make yourself an ark of cypress wood; make rooms in it and coat it with pitch inside and out. . . . But I will establish my covenant with you, and you will enter the ark—you and your sons and your wife and your sons' wives with you. You are to bring into the ark two of all living creatures, male and female, to keep them alive with you. Two of every kind of bird, of every kind of animal and of every kind of creature that moves along the ground will come to you to be kept alive. You are to take every kind of food that is to be eaten and store it away as food for you and for them."

Noah did everything just as God commanded him. . . .

In the six hundredth year of Noah's life, on the seventeenth day of the second month—on that day all the springs of the great deep burst forth, and the floodgates of the heavens were opened. And rain fell on the earth forty days and forty nights. . . .

Every living thing on the face of the earth was wiped out; men and animals and the creatures that move along the ground and the birds of the air were wiped from the earth. Only Noah was left, and those with him in the ark.

The waters flooded the earth for a hundred and fifty days.

But God remembered Noah and all the wild animals and the livestock that were with him in the ark, and he sent a wind over the earth, and the waters receded. . . .

By the first day of the first month of Noah's six hundred and first year, the water had dried up from the earth. Noah then removed the covering from the ark and saw that the surface of the ground was dry. By the twenty-seventh day of the second month the earth was completely dry. . . .

So Noah came out, together with his sons and his wife and his sons' wives. All the animals and all the creatures that move along the ground and all the birds—everything that moves on the earth—came out of the ark, one kind after another.

Then Noah built an altar to the LORD and, taking some of all the clean animals and clean birds, he sacrificed burnt offerings on it. The LORD smelled the pleasing aroma and said in his heart: "Never again will I curse the ground because of man, even though every inclination of his heart is evil from childhood. And never again will I destroy all living creatures, as I have done.

   As long as the earth endures, seedtime and harvest, cold and heat, summer and winter, day and night will never cease."

   —from Genesis 6:5–8:22 (NIV)

Get wisdom! Get understanding! Do not forget, nor turn away from the words of my mouth. Do not forsake her, and she will preserve you; love her, and she will keep you. Wisdom is the principal thing; therefore get wisdom. And in all your getting, get understanding.

> —*Proverbs 4:5–7 (NKJV)*

Instruct the wise, and they will be even wiser. Teach the righteous, and they will learn even more.

> —*Proverbs 9:9 (NLT)*

Wise people store up knowledge, but the mouth of the foolish is near destruction.

> —*Proverbs 10:14 (NKJV)*

How much better to get wisdom than
gold, to choose understanding rather
than silver!
        —*Proverbs 16:16 (NIV)*

Intelligent people are always ready
to learn. Their ears are open for
knowledge.
        —*Proverbs 18:15 (NLT)*

Truth, wisdom, learning, and
understanding are worth paying money
for. And they are worth far too much to
ever sell.
        —*Proverbs 23:23 (ERV)*

The integrity of the upright will
guide them, but the perversity of the
unfaithful will destroy them.
        —*Proverbs 11:3 (NKJV)*

Do not be wise in your own eyes; fear
the LORD and shun evil.
        —*Proverbs 3:7 (NIV)*

The instructions of the LORD are perfect, reviving the soul. The decrees of the LORD are trustworthy, making wise the simple.

—*Psalm 19:7 (NLT)*

But the wisdom that is from above is first pure, then peaceable, gentle, willing to yield, full of mercy and good fruits, without partiality and without hypocrisy.

—*James 3:17 (NKJV)*

A wise person obeys when someone tells him to do something. But a fool argues and brings trouble to himself.

—*Proverbs 10:8 (ERV)*

Who is like the wise man? Who knows the explanation of things? Wisdom brightens a man's face and changes its hard appearance.

—*Ecclesiastes 8:1 (NIV)*

Fear of the LORD is the foundation of true wisdom. All who obey his commandments will grow in wisdom. Praise him forever!
  —*Psalm 111:10 (NLT)*

In the multitude of words sin is not lacking, but he who restrains his lips is wise.
  —*Proverbs 10:19 (NKJV)*

My purpose is that they may be encouraged in heart and united in love, so that they may have the full riches of complete understanding, in order that they may know the mystery of God, namely, Christ, in whom are hidden all the treasures of wisdom and knowledge.
  —*Colossians 2:2–3 (NIV)*

Wisdom makes one wise man more powerful than ten rulers in a city.
  —*Ecclesiastes 7:19 (NIV)*

Lord, your commands make me wiser than my enemies. Your law is with me always.

—*Psalm 119:98 (ERV)*

For the LORD gives wisdom; from His mouth come knowledge and understanding.

—*Proverbs 2:6 (NKJV)*

If you are wise and understand God's ways, prove it by living an honorable life, doing good works with the humility that comes from wisdom.

—*James 3:13 (NLT)*

Be very careful, then, how you live—not as unwise but as wise.

—*Ephesians 5:15 (NIV)*

He who walks with wise men will be wise, but the companion of fools will be destroyed.

—*Proverbs 13:20 (NKJV)*

A few words quietly spoken by a wise man are much better than words shouted by a foolish ruler. Wisdom is better than swords and spears in war. But one foolish person can destroy much good.

—*Ecclesiastes 9:17–18 (ERV)*

Wisdom is even better when you have money. Both are a benefit as you go through life. Wisdom and money can get you almost anything, but only wisdom can save your life.

—*Ecclesiastes 7:11–12 (NLT)*

Wisdom makes a man more powerful. Knowledge gives a man strength.

—*Proverbs 24:5 (ERV)*

If you need wisdom, ask our generous God, and he will give it to you. He will not rebuke you for asking.

—*James 1:5 (NLT)*

At Gibeon the LORD appeared to
Solomon in a dream by night; and God
said, "Ask! What shall I give you?"

And Solomon said: "You have shown
great mercy to Your servant David
my father, because he walked before
You in truth, in righteousness, and
in uprightness of heart with You; You
have continued this great kindness for
him, and You have given him a son to
sit on his throne, as it is this day. Now,
O LORD my God, You have made Your
servant king instead of my father David,
but I am a little child; I do not know
how to go out or come in. And Your
servant is in the midst of Your people
whom You have chosen, a great people,
too numerous to be numbered or
counted. Therefore give to Your servant

an understanding heart to judge Your people, that I may discern between good and evil. For who is able to judge this great people of Yours?"

The speech pleased the Lord, that Solomon had asked this thing. Then God said to him: "Because you have asked this thing, and have not asked long life for yourself, nor have asked riches for yourself, nor have asked the life of your enemies, but have asked for yourself understanding to discern justice, behold, I have done according to your words; see, I have given you a wise and understanding heart, so that there has not been anyone like you before you, nor shall any like you arise after you. And I have also given you what you have not asked: both riches and honor, so that there shall not be anyone like you among the kings all your days. So if you walk in

My ways, to keep My statutes and My commandments, as your father David walked, then I will lengthen your days."

Then Solomon awoke; and indeed it had been a dream. And he came to Jerusalem and stood before the ark of the covenant of the LORD, offered up burnt offerings, offered peace offerings, and made a feast for all his servants.
—*1 Kings 3:5–15 (NKJV)*

True CONTENTMENT

The fear of the LORD leads to life, and
he who has it will abide in satisfaction;
He will not be visited with evil.
    —*Proverbs 19:23 (NKJV)*

Now godliness with contentment is
great gain. For we brought nothing
into this world, and it is certain we can
carry nothing out. And having food and
clothing, with these we shall be content.
But those who desire to be rich fall into
temptation and a snare, and into many
foolish and harmful lusts which drown
men in destruction and perdition. For
the love of money is a root of all kinds
of evil, for which some have strayed
from the faith in their greediness, and
pierced themselves through with many
sorrows.
    —*1 Timothy 6:6–10 (NKJV)*

Therefore I tell you, do not worry about your life, what you will eat or drink; or about your body, what you will wear. Is not life more important than food, and the body more important than clothes? Look at the birds of the air; they do not sow or reap or store away in barns, and yet your heavenly Father feeds them. Are you not much more valuable than they? Who of you by worrying can add a single hour to his life?
　　—Matthew 6:25–27 (NIV)

No one can serve two masters. Either he will hate the one and love the other, or he will be devoted to the one and despise the other. You cannot serve both God and Money.
　　—Matthew 6:24 (NIV)

So if we have enough food and clothing, let us be content.
　　—1 Timothy 6:8 (NLT)

And I have been a constant example
of how you can help those in need by
working hard. You should remember
the words of the Lord Jesus: "It is more
blessed to give than to receive."
  —*Acts 20:35 (NLT)*

Now, if you will be careful to obey
the Lord your God and follow all his
commands that I tell you today, then
the Lord your God will put you high
above all the nations on earth.
  —*Deuteronomy 28:1 (ERV)*

Not that I speak in regard to need, for
I have learned in whatever state I am,
to be content: I know how to be abased,
and I know how to abound. Everywhere
and in all things I have learned both
to be full and to be hungry, both to
abound and to suffer need.
  —*Philippians 4:11–12 (NKJV)*

Keep your lives free from the love of money and be content with what you have, because God has said, "Never will I leave you; never will I forsake you."
    —*Hebrews 13:5 (NIV)*

My soul, praise the Lord! And don't forget that he is truly kind. . . . God gives us plenty of good things. He makes us young again, like an eagle.
    —*Psalm 103:2, 5 (ERV)*

Don't store up treasures here on earth, where moths eat them and rust destroys them, and where thieves break in and steal. Store your treasures in heaven, where moths and rust cannot destroy, and thieves do not break in and steal. Wherever your treasure is, there the desires of your heart will also be.
    —*Matthew 6:19–21 (NLT)*

CHARACTER PORTRAIT

JOB UNDERSTANDS *Ownership*

In the land of Uz there lived a man whose name was Job. This man was blameless and upright; he feared God and shunned evil. He had seven sons and three daughters, and he owned seven thousand sheep, three thousand camels, five hundred yoke of oxen and five hundred donkeys, and had a large number of servants. He was the greatest man among all the people of the East.

His sons used to take turns holding feasts in their homes, and they would invite their three sisters to eat and drink with them. When a period of feasting had run its course, Job would send and have them purified. Early in the morning he would sacrifice a burnt

offering for each of them, thinking, "Perhaps my children have sinned and cursed God in their hearts." This was Job's regular custom.

One day the angels came to present themselves before the LORD, and Satan also came with them. The LORD said to Satan, "Where have you come from?"

Satan answered the LORD, "From roaming through the earth and going back and forth in it."

Then the LORD said to Satan, "Have you considered my servant Job? There is no one on earth like him; he is blameless and upright, a man who fears God and shuns evil."

"Does Job fear God for nothing?" Satan replied. "Have you not put a hedge around him and his household and everything he has? You have blessed the work of his hands, so that his flocks and herds are spread throughout the land. But stretch out your hand and strike everything he has, and he will surely curse you to your face."

The LORD said to Satan, "Very well, then, everything he has is in your hands, but on the man himself do not lay a finger."

Then Satan went out from the presence of the LORD.

One day when Job's sons and daughters were feasting and drinking wine at the oldest brother's house, a messenger came to Job and said, "The oxen were plowing and the donkeys were grazing nearby, and the Sabeans attacked and carried them off. They put the servants to the sword, and I am the only one who has escaped to tell you!"

While he was still speaking, another messenger came and said, "The fire of God fell from the sky and burned up the sheep and the servants, and I am the only one who has escaped to tell you!"

While he was still speaking, another messenger came and said, "The Chaldeans formed three raiding parties and swept down on your camels and carried them off. They put the servants to the sword, and I am the only one who has escaped to tell you!"

While he was still speaking, yet another messenger came and said, "Your sons and daughters were feasting and drinking wine at the oldest brother's house, when suddenly a mighty wind swept in from the desert and struck the four corners of the house. It collapsed on them and they are dead, and I am the only one who has escaped to tell you!"

At this, Job got up and tore his robe and shaved his head. Then he fell to

the ground in worship and said: "Naked
I came from my mother's womb, and
naked I will depart. The LORD gave and
the LORD has taken away; may the
name of the LORD be praised."
In all this, Job did not sin by charging
God with wrongdoing.

—*Job 1:1–22 (NIV)*

The Strength TO RESIST TEMPTATION

No temptation has overtaken you except such as is common to man; but God is faithful, who will not allow you to be tempted beyond what you are able, but with the temptation will also make the way of escape, that you may be able to bear it.

—*1 Corinthians 10:13 (NKJV)*

Brothers and sisters, a person in your group might do something wrong. You people who are spiritual should go to the person who is sinning. You should help to make him right again. You should do this in a gentle way. But be careful! You might be tempted to sin, too.

—*Galatians 6:1 (ERV)*

He who pursues righteousness and love finds life, prosperity and honor.
　　—Proverbs 21:21 (NIV)

Since he himself has gone through suffering and testing, he is able to help us when we are being tested.
　　—Hebrews 2:18 (NLT)

Jesus, the high priest that we have, is able to understand our weaknesses. When Jesus lived on earth, he was tempted in every way. He was tempted in the same ways that we are tempted, but he never sinned.
　　—Hebrews 4:15 (ERV)

And forgive us our sins, for we also forgive everyone who is indebted to us. And do not lead us into temptation, but deliver us from the evil one.
　　—Luke 11:4 (NKJV)

When tempted, no one should say, "God is tempting me." For God cannot be tempted by evil, nor does he tempt anyone; but each one is tempted when, by his own evil desire, he is dragged away and enticed.

—*James 1:13–14 (NIV)*

Watch and pray so that you will not fall into temptation. The spirit is willing, but the body is weak.

—*Matthew 26:41 (NIV)*

Jesus said to them, "Why are you sleeping? Get up and pray for strength against temptation."

—*Luke 22:46 (ERV)*

Godliness guards the path of the blameless, but the evil are misled by sin.

—*Proverbs 13:6 (NLT)*

The righteousness of the blameless
makes a straight way for them, but the
wicked are brought down by their own
wickedness.
  —*Proverbs 11:5 (NIV)*

I traverse the way of righteousness, in
the midst of the paths of justice.
  —*Proverbs 8:20 (NKJV)*

It is better to gain only a little the
right way than to gain much through
cheating.
  —*Proverbs 16:8 (ERV)*

Consecrate yourselves therefore, and
be holy, for I am the LORD your God.
And you shall keep My statutes, and
perform them: I am the LORD who
sanctifies you.
  —*Leviticus 20:7–8 (NKJV)*

Submit yourselves, then, to God. Resist the devil, and he will flee from you.
—*James 4:7 (NIV)*

You must be holy because I, the LORD, am holy. I have set you apart from all other people to be my very own.
—*Leviticus 20:26 (NLT)*

Make every effort to live in peace with all men and to be holy; without holiness no one will see the Lord.
—*Hebrews 12:14 (NIV)*

The northern king will use lies and smooth talking to trick the Jews that quit following the holy agreement. Those Jews will sin even worse. But the Jews that know God and obey him will be strong. They will fight back!
—*Daniel 11:32 (ERV)*

To reject the law is to praise the wicked; to obey the law is to fight them.
—*Proverbs 28:4 (NLT)*

But now you must be holy in everything you do, just as God who chose you is holy. For the Scriptures say, "You must be holy because I am holy."
—*1 Peter 1:15–16 (NLT)*

And lead us not into temptation, but deliver us from the evil one.
—*Matthew 6:13 (NIV)*

Watch and pray, lest you enter into temptation. The spirit indeed is willing, but the flesh is weak.
—*Mark 14:38 (NKJV)*

For our heart shall rejoice in Him, because we have trusted in His holy name.
—*Psalm 33:21 (NKJV)*

CHARACTER PORTRAIT
DANIEL AND HIS FRIENDS *Resist* TEMPTATION

Then the king ordered Ashpenaz, chief of his court officials, to bring in some of the Israelites from the royal family and the nobility—young men without any physical defect, handsome, showing aptitude for every kind of learning, well informed, quick to understand, and qualified to serve in the king's palace. He was to teach them the language and literature of the Babylonians. The king assigned them a daily amount of food and wine from the king's table. They were to be trained for three years, and after that they were to enter the king's service.

Among these were some from Judah: Daniel, Hananiah, Mishael and Azariah. The chief official gave them new names: to Daniel, the name Belteshazzar;

to Hananiah, Shadrach; to Mishael, Meshach; and to Azariah, Abednego.

But Daniel resolved not to defile himself with the royal food and wine, and he asked the chief official for permission not to defile himself this way. Now God had caused the official to show favor and sympathy to Daniel, but the official told Daniel, "I am afraid of my lord the king, who has assigned your food and drink. Why should he see you looking worse than the other young men your age? The king would then have my head because of you."

Daniel then said to the guard whom the chief official had appointed over Daniel, Hananiah, Mishael and Azariah, "Please test your servants for ten days: Give us nothing but vegetables to eat and water to drink. Then compare our appearance with that of the young men who eat the royal food, and treat your servants in accordance with what you see." So he agreed to this and tested them for ten days.

At the end of the ten days they looked healthier and better nourished than any of the young men who ate the royal food. So the guard took away their choice food and the wine they were to drink and gave them vegetables instead.

—*Daniel 1:3–16 (NIV)*

Gracious SERVANTHOOD

Each of you received a spiritual gift
from God. God has shown you his
grace (kindness) in many different
ways. And you are like servants who
are responsible for using God's gifts. So
be good servants and use your gifts to
serve each other.
>   —*1 Peter 4:10 (ERV)*

Serve wholeheartedly, as if you were
serving the Lord, not men.
>   —*Ephesians 6:7 (NIV)*

For you have been called to live in
freedom, my brothers and sisters.
But don't use your freedom to satisfy
your sinful nature. Instead, use your
freedom to serve one another in love.
>   —*Galatians 5:13 (NLT)*

Be kindly affectionate to one another with brotherly love, in honor giving preference to one another; not lagging in diligence, fervent in spirit, serving the Lord.

—*Romans 12:10–11 (NKJV)*

This service that you perform is not only supplying the needs of God's people but is also overflowing in many expressions of thanks to God. Because of the service by which you have proved yourselves, men will praise God for the obedience that accompanies your confession of the gospel of Christ, and for your generosity in sharing with them and with everyone else.

—*2 Corinthians 9:12–13 (NIV)*

For even the Son of Man did not come to be served, but to serve, and to give his life as a ransom for many.

—*Mark 10:45 (NIV)*

Jesus answered, "It is written in the Scriptures: 'You must worship the Lord your God. Serve only him!'"
—*Luke 4:8 (ERV)*

These were his instructions to them: "You must always act in the fear of the LORD, with faithfulness and an undivided heart."
—*2 Chronicles 19:9 (NLT)*

But now, by dying to what once bound us, we have been released from the law so that we serve in the new way of the Spirit, and not in the old way of the written code.
—*Romans 7:6 (NIV)*

Anyone who wants to be my disciple must follow me, because my servants must be where I am. And the Father will honor anyone who serves me.
—*John 12:26 (NLT)*

In all the work you are doing, work the best you can. Work like you are working for the Lord, not for people. Remember that you will receive your reward from the Lord. He will give you what he promised his people. You are serving the Lord Christ.

—*Colossians 3:23–24 (ERV)*

And whoever gives one of these little ones only a cup of cold water in the name of a disciple, assuredly, I say to you, he shall by no means lose his reward.

—*Matthew 10:42 (NKJV)*

Now these are the gifts Christ gave to the church: the apostles, the prophets, the evangelists, and the pastors and teachers. Their responsibility is to equip God's people to do his work and build up the church, the body of Christ.

—*Ephesians 4:11–12 (NLT)*

In your lives you must think and act like Christ Jesus. Christ himself was like God in everything. Christ was equal with God. But Christ did not think that being equal with God was something that he must keep. He gave up his place with God and agreed to be like a servant. He was born to be a man and became like a servant.
—*Philippians 2:5–7 (ERV)*

Those persons who serve in a good way are making an honorable place for themselves. And they will feel very sure of their faith in Christ Jesus.
—*1 Timothy 3:13 (ERV)*

CHARACTER PORTRAIT
JESUS WAS A SERVANT *Leader*

Jesus knew that the Father had given him authority over everything and that he had come from God and would return to God. So he got up from the table, took off his robe, wrapped a towel around his waist, and poured water into a basin. Then he began to wash the disciples' feet, drying them with the towel he had around him.

When Jesus came to Simon Peter, Peter said to him, "Lord, are you going to wash my feet?"

Jesus replied, "You don't understand now what I am doing, but someday you will."

"No," Peter protested, "you will never ever wash my feet!"

Jesus replied, "Unless I wash you, you won't belong to me."

Simon Peter exclaimed, "Then wash my hands and head as well, Lord, not just my feet!"

Jesus replied, "A person who has bathed all over does not need to wash, except for the feet, to be entirely clean. And you disciples are clean, but not all of you." For Jesus knew who would betray him. That is what he meant when he said, "Not all of you are clean."

After washing their feet, he put on his robe again and sat down and asked, "Do you understand what I was doing? You call me 'Teacher' and 'Lord,' and you are right, because that's what I am. And since I, your Lord and Teacher, have washed your feet, you ought to wash each other's feet. I have given you an example to follow. Do as I have done to you."

—*John 13:3–15 (NLT)*

Reliability

He who is faithful in what is least is faithful also in much; and he who is unjust in what is least is unjust also in much.

—Luke 16:10 (NKJV)

Kings take pleasure in honest lips; they value a man who speaks the truth.

—Proverbs 16:13 (NIV)

Do all you can to live a peaceful life. Take care of your own business. Do your own work. We have already told you to do these things.

—1 Thessalonians 4:11 (ERV)

Work brings profit, but mere talk leads to poverty!

—Proverbs 14:23 (NLT)

Wealth gained by dishonesty will be diminished, but he who gathers by labor will increase.
    —*Proverbs 13:11 (NKJV)*

If a person is skilled in his work, then he is good enough to serve kings. He will not have to work for people who are not important.
    —*Proverbs 22:29 (ERV)*

She considers a field and buys it; from her profits she plants a vineyard. She girds herself with strength, and strengthens her arms.
    —*Proverbs 31:16–17 (NKJV)*

A man can do nothing better than to eat and drink and find satisfaction in his work. This too, I see, is from the hand of God.
    —*Ecclesiastes 2:24 (NIV)*

Darius the Mede decided to divide the kingdom into 120 provinces, and he appointed a high officer to rule over each province. The king also chose Daniel and two others as administrators to supervise the high officers and protect the king's interests. Daniel soon proved himself more capable than all the other administrators and high officers. Because of Daniel's great ability, the king made plans to place him over the entire empire.

—Daniel 6:1–3 (NLT)

CHARACTER PORTRAIT
JOSEPH WAS RELIABLE IN *Every* CIRCUMSTANCE

When Joseph was taken to Egypt by the Ishmaelite traders, he was purchased by Potiphar, an Egyptian officer. Potiphar was captain of the guard for Pharaoh, the king of Egypt.

The LORD was with Joseph, so he succeeded in everything he did as he served in the home of his Egyptian master. Potiphar noticed this and realized that the LORD was with Joseph, giving him success in everything he did. This pleased Potiphar, so he soon made Joseph his personal attendant. He put him in charge of his entire household and everything he owned. From the day Joseph was put in charge of his master's household and property, the LORD began to bless Potiphar's household for Joseph's sake. All his household affairs ran smoothly, and his crops and livestock flourished. So Potiphar gave Joseph complete administrative responsibility over everything he owned. With Joseph there, he didn't worry about a thing— except what kind of food to eat!

Joseph was a very handsome and well-built young man, and Potiphar's wife soon began to look at him lustfully. "Come and sleep with me," she demanded.

But Joseph refused. "Look," he told her, "my master trusts me with everything in his entire household. No one here has more authority than I do. He has held back nothing from me except you, because you are his wife. How could I do such a wicked thing? It would be a great sin against God."

She kept putting pressure on Joseph day after day, but he refused to sleep with her, and he kept out of her way as much as possible. One day, however, no one else was around when he went in to do his work. She came and grabbed him by his cloak, demanding, "Come on, sleep with me!" Joseph tore himself away, but he left his cloak in her hand as he ran from the house.

When she saw that she was holding his cloak and he had fled, she called out to her servants. Soon all the men came running. "Look!" she said. "My husband has brought this Hebrew slave here to make fools of us! He came into my room to rape me, but I screamed. When he heard me scream, he ran outside and got away, but he left his cloak behind with me."

She kept the cloak with her until

her husband came home. Then she told him her story. "That Hebrew slave you've brought into our house tried to come in and fool around with me," she said. "But when I screamed, he ran outside, leaving his cloak with me!"

Potiphar was furious when he heard his wife's story about how Joseph had treated her. So he took Joseph and threw him into the prison where the king's prisoners were held, and there he remained. But the LORD was with Joseph in the prison and showed him his faithful love. And the LORD made Joseph a favorite with the prison warden. Before long, the warden put Joseph in charge of all the other prisoners and over everything that happened in the prison. The warden had no more worries, because Joseph took care of everything. The LORD was

with him and caused everything he
did to succeed.

   —Genesis 39:1–23 (NLT)

A *Humble* HEART

He teaches humble people his ways. He leads them with fairness.
—*Psalm 25:9 (ERV)*

The LORD lifts up the humble; He casts the wicked down to the ground.
—*Psalm 147:6 (NKJV)*

Young men, in the same way be submissive to those who are older. All of you, clothe yourselves with humility toward one another, because, "God opposes the proud but gives grace to the humble." Humble yourselves, therefore, under God's mighty hand, that he may lift you up in due time.
—*1 Peter 5:5–6 (NIV)*

For the LORD takes delight in his people; he crowns the humble with salvation.
> —*Psalm 149:4 (NIV)*

When you do things, don't let selfishness or pride be your guide. Be humble and give more honor to other people than to yourselves.
> —*Philippians 2:3 (ERV)*

Take my yoke upon you. Let me teach you, because I am humble and gentle at heart, and you will find rest for your souls.
> —*Matthew 11:29 (NLT)*

Finally, all of you, live in harmony with one another; be sympathetic, love as brothers, be compassionate and humble.
> —*1 Peter 3:8 (NIV)*

Walk worthy of the calling with which you were called, with all lowliness and gentleness, with longsuffering, bearing with one another in love.

—Ephesians 4:1–2 (NKJV)

Humble yourselves before the Lord, and he will lift you up in honor.

—James 4:10 (NLT)

If a person is proud and makes fun of other people, the Lord will punish him and make fun of him. But the Lord is kind to humble people.

—Proverbs 3:34 (ERV)

Then he said to me, "Do not fear, Daniel, for from the first day that you set your heart to understand, and to humble yourself before your God, your words were heard; and I have come because of your words."

—Daniel 10:12 (NKJV)

Humility and the fear of the LORD bring wealth and honor and life.

—*Proverbs 22:4 (NIV)*

Man, the Lord told you what goodness is. This is what the Lord wants from you: Be fair to other people. Love kindness and loyalty. Live humbly with your God. Don't try to impress him with gifts.

—*Micah 6:8 (ERV)*

So anyone who becomes as humble as this little child is the greatest in the Kingdom of Heaven.

—*Matthew 18:4 (NLT)*

Therefore, as God's chosen people, holy and dearly loved, clothe yourselves with compassion, kindness, humility, gentleness and patience.

—*Colossians 3:12 (NIV)*

Let your gentleness be known to all men. The Lord is at hand.

—*Philippians 4:5 (NKJV)*

But you should keep the Lord Christ holy in your hearts. Always be ready to answer every person who asks you to explain about the hope you have.

—*1 Peter 3:15 (ERV)*

CHARACTER PORTRAIT
MOSES, A GREAT AND *Humble* MAN

Now Moses was a very humble man,
more humble than anyone else on the
face of the earth.
>   —*Numbers 12:3 (NIV)*

One day Moses was tending the flock
of his father-in-law, Jethro, the priest
of Midian. He led the flock far into
the wilderness and came to Sinai, the
mountain of God. There the angel of
the LORD appeared to him in a blazing
fire from the middle of a bush. Moses
stared in amazement. Though the bush
was engulfed in flames, it didn't burn
up. "This is amazing," Moses said to
himself. "Why isn't that bush burning
up? I must go see it."

When the LORD saw Moses coming to
take a closer look, God called to him
from the middle of the bush, "Moses!

Moses!"

"Here I am!" Moses replied.

"Do not come any closer," the LORD
warned. "Take off your sandals, for
you are standing on holy ground. I
am the God of your father—the God
of Abraham, the God of Isaac, and the
God of Jacob." When Moses heard this,
he covered his face because he was
afraid to look at God.

Then the LORD told him, "I have
certainly seen the oppression of my
people in Egypt. I have heard their
cries of distress because of their harsh
slave drivers. Yes, I am aware of their
suffering. . . . Now go, for I am sending
you to Pharaoh. You must lead my
people Israel out of Egypt."

But Moses protested to God, "Who
am I to appear before Pharaoh? Who
am I to lead the people of Israel out of
Egypt?"

God answered, "I will be with you. And this is your sign that I am the one who has sent you: When you have brought the people out of Egypt, you will worship God at this very mountain."

—*Exodus 3:1–7, 10–12 (NLT)*

But Moses said to the Lord, "But Lord, I am telling you the truth, I am not a skilled speaker. I have never been able to speak well. And now, even after talking to you, I am still not a good speaker. You know that I talk slowly and don't use the best words."

Then the Lord said to him, "Who made a person's mouth? And who can make a person deaf or not able to speak? Who can make a person blind? Who can make a person able to see? I am the One who can do all these things—I am YAHWEH. So go. I will be with you when you speak. I will give you the words to say."

But Moses said, "My Lord, I beg you to send another person—not me."

Then the Lord became angry with Moses and said, "Fine! I'll give you someone to help you. I will use your brother Aaron, from the family of Levi. He is a skilled speaker. Aaron is already coming to see you. He will be happy to see you. He will go with you to Pharaoh. I will tell you what to say. Then you will tell Aaron, and Aaron will choose the right words to speak to Pharaoh."

—*Exodus 4:10–15 (ERV)*

BUILDING

Character

For the LORD grants wisdom! From his mouth come knowledge and understanding.

—Proverbs 2:6 (NLT)

 # *Love* GOD

Oh, love the LORD, all you His saints!
For the LORD preserves the faithful,
and fully repays the proud person.
    —*Psalm 31:23 (NKJV)*

Jesus replied: "Love the Lord your God
with all your heart and with all your
soul and with all your mind."
    —*Matthew 22:37 (NIV)*

If a person knows my commands and
obeys those commands, then that
person truly loves me. And my Father
will love the person that loves me. And I
will love that person. I will show myself
to him.
    —*John 14:21 (ERV)*

We love each other because he loved us first.
—*1 John 4:19 (NLT)*

Jesus replied, "If anyone loves me, he will obey my teaching. My Father will love him, and we will come to him and make our home with him."
—*John 14:23 (NIV)*

Therefore take careful heed to yourselves, that you love the LORD your God.
—*Joshua 23:11 (NKJV)*

And loving means living the way he commanded us to live. And God's command is this: that you live a life of love. You heard this command from the beginning.
—*2 John 1:6 (ERV)*

CHARACTER PORTRAIT
PETER LIVED HIS *Love* FOR GOD

Then Peter stood up with the other
eleven apostles. He spoke loudly so that
all the people could hear. He said, "My
Jewish brothers and all of you who live
in Jerusalem, listen to me. I will tell you
something you need to know. Listen
carefully. . . . My Jewish brothers,
listen to these words: Jesus from
Nazareth was a very special man. God
clearly showed this to you. God proved
this by the powerful and amazing
things he did through Jesus. You all
saw these things. So you know this is
true. Jesus was given to you, and you
killed him. With the help of bad men
you nailed Jesus to a cross. But God
knew all this would happen. This was
God's plan. God made this plan long
ago. Jesus suffered the pain of death,

but God made him free. God raised
Jesus from death. Death could not hold
Jesus. . . . So, all the Jewish people
should know this truly: God has made
Jesus to be Lord and Christ. He is the
man you nailed to the cross!"

When the people heard this, they felt
very, very sorry. They asked Peter and
the other apostles, "Brothers, what
should we do?"

Peter said to them, "Change your
hearts and lives and be baptized, each
one of you, in the name of Jesus Christ.
Then God will forgive your sins, and
you will receive the gift of the Holy
Spirit. This promise is for you. It is also
for your children and for the people
that are far away. It is for every person
that the Lord our God calls to himself."

Peter warned them with many
other words; he begged them, "Save
yourselves from the evil of the people

that live now!" Then those people who accepted (believed) what Peter said were baptized. On that day about 3,000 people were added to the group of believers.

> —*from Acts 2:14, 22–24, 36–41 (ERV)*

So when they had eaten breakfast,
Jesus said to Simon Peter, "Simon, son
of Jonah, do you love Me more than
these?"

He said to Him, "Yes, Lord; You know
that I love You."

He said to him, "Feed My lambs."

He said to him again a second time,
"Simon, son of Jonah, do you love Me?"

He said to Him, "Yes, Lord; You know
that I love You."

He said to him, "Tend My sheep."

He said to him the third time, "Simon,
son of Jonah, do you love Me?" Peter
was grieved because He said to him the
third time, "Do you love Me?"

And he said to Him, "Lord, You know
all things; You know that I love You."

Jesus said to him, "Feed My sheep."
—*John 21:15–17 (NKJV)*

So look at Apollos and me as mere servants of Christ who have been put in charge of explaining God's mysteries. Now, a person who is put in charge as a manager must be faithful.

—*1 Corinthians 4:1–2 (NLT)*

I tell you the truth, anyone who has faith in me will do what I have been doing. He will do even greater things than these, because I am going to the Father.

—*John 14:12 (NIV)*

God will do this, for he is faithful to do what he says, and he has invited you into partnership with his Son, Jesus Christ our Lord.

—*1 Corinthians 1:9 (NLT)*

Watch, stand fast in the faith, be brave, be strong.
>—*1 Corinthians 16:13 (NKJV)*

Create in me a pure heart, O God, and renew a steadfast spirit within me.
>—*Psalm 51:10 (NIV)*

Solomon answered [God], "You were very kind to your servant, my father David. He followed you. He was good and lived right. And you showed the greatest kindness to him when you allowed his son to rule on his throne after him."
>—*1 Kings 3:6 (ERV)*

In this way, King Hezekiah handled the distribution throughout all Judah, doing what was pleasing and good in the sight of the LORD his God.
>—*2 Chronicles 31:20 (NLT)*

Therefore, my dear friends, as you have always obeyed—not only in my presence, but now much more in my absence—continue to work out your salvation with fear and trembling.

—*Philippians 2:12 (NIV)*

So Jesus said to them, "Because of your unbelief; for assuredly, I say to you, if you have faith as a mustard seed, you will say to this mountain, 'Move from here to there,' and it will move; and nothing will be impossible for you."

—*Matthew 17:20 (NKJV)*

We have been made right with God because of our faith. So we have peace with God through our Lord Jesus Christ.

—*Romans 5:1 (ERV)*

My teaching and my speaking were not with wise words that persuade people. But the proof of my teaching was the power that the Spirit gives. I did this so that your faith would be in God's power, not in the wisdom of a man.

—*1 Corinthians 2:4–5 (ERV)*

Be strong and very courageous. Be careful to obey all the law my servant Moses gave you; do not turn from it to the right or to the left, that you may be successful wherever you go.

—*Joshua 1:7 (NIV)*

Flee also youthful lusts; but pursue righteousness, faith, love, peace with those who call on the Lord out of a pure heart.

—*2 Timothy 2:22 (NKJV)*

To the faithful you show yourself faithful; to those with integrity you show integrity.

      —2 Samuel 22:26 (NLT)

Let no one despise your youth, but be an example to the believers in word, in conduct, in love, in spirit, in faith, in purity.

      —1 Timothy 4:12 (NKJV)

For the LORD loves the just and will not forsake his faithful ones. They will be protected forever, but the offspring of the wicked will be cut off.

      —Psalm 37:28 (NIV)

He stores up sound wisdom for the upright; He is a shield to those who walk uprightly; He guards the paths of justice, and preserves the way of His saints.

      —Proverbs 2:7–8 (NKJV)

Brothers and sisters, continue to think about the things that are good and worthy of praise. Think about the things that are true and honorable and right and pure and beautiful and respected.

—*Philippians 4:8 (ERV)*

Faith means being sure of the things we hope for. And faith means knowing that something is real even if we don't see it. God was pleased with those people who lived a long time ago, because they had faith like this.

Faith helps us understand that God created the whole world with his command. This means that the things we see were made by something that cannot be seen.

Cain and Abel both offered sacrifices to God. But Abel offered a better sacrifice to God because Abel had faith. God said he was pleased with the things Abel offered. And so God called Abel a good man because Abel had faith. Abel died, but through his faith he is still speaking.

Enoch was carried away from this earth. He never died. The Scripture says that, before Enoch was carried off, he was a man who truly pleased God. Later, people could not find Enoch, because God took Enoch to be with him. This happened to Enoch because he had faith. Without faith, a person cannot please God. Any person who comes to God must believe that God is real. And any person who comes to God must believe that God rewards those people who truly want to find him.

Noah was warned by God about things that Noah could not yet see. But Noah had faith and respect for God. So Noah built a large boat to save his family. With his faith, Noah showed that the world was wrong. And Noah became one of those people who are made right with God through faith.

God called Abraham to travel to

another place that God promised
to give Abraham. Abraham did not
know where that other place was.
But Abraham obeyed God and started
traveling, because Abraham had faith.
Abraham lived in that country that God
promised to give him. Abraham lived
there like a visitor who did not belong.
Abraham did this because he had faith.
Abraham lived in tents with Isaac and
Jacob. Isaac and Jacob also received
that same promise from God. Abraham
was waiting for the city that has real
foundations. He was waiting for the city
that is planned and built by God.

   Abraham was too old to have
children. And Sarah was not able to
have children. But Abraham had faith
in God, and so God made them able to
have children. Abraham trusted God to
do the things he promised. This man
was so old that he was almost dead.

But from that one man came as many descendants (people) as there are stars in the sky. So many people came from that one man that they are like grains of sand on the seashore.

All those great men continued living with faith until they died. Those men did not get the things that God promised his people. The men only saw those things coming far in the future and were glad. Those men accepted the fact that they were like visitors and strangers on earth.

—*Hebrews 11:1–13 (ERV)*

Therefore, holy brethren, partakers of the heavenly calling, consider the Apostle and High Priest of our confession, Christ Jesus, who was faithful to Him who appointed Him, as Moses also was faithful in all His house. For this One has been counted worthy of more glory than Moses, inasmuch as He who built the house has more honor than the house. For every house is built by someone, but He who built all things is God. And Moses indeed was faithful in all His house as a servant, for a testimony of those things which would be spoken afterward, but Christ as a Son over His own house, whose house we are if we hold fast the confidence and the rejoicing of the hope firm to the end.

—Hebrews 3:1–6 (NKJV)

Oh, the joys of those who do not follow
the advice of the wicked, or stand
around with sinners, or join in with
mockers. But they delight in the law
of the LORD, meditating on it day and
night.

> —*Psalm 1:1–2 (NLT)*

We believe in you. We know that you
are the Holy One from God.

> —*John 6:69 (ERV)*

Teach me knowledge and good
judgment, for I believe in your
commands.

> —*Psalm 119:66 (NIV)*

"The time promised by God has come at last!" [Jesus] announced. "The Kingdom of God is near! Repent of your sins and believe the Good News!"
— *Mark 1:15 (NLT)*

Jesus said to her, "I am the resurrection and the life. He who believes in me will live, even though he dies; and whoever lives and believes in me will never die. Do you believe this?"
— *John 11:25–26 (NIV)*

Though now you do not see Him, yet believing, you rejoice with joy inexpressible and full of glory.
— *1 Peter 1:8 (NKJV)*

Through him you believe in God, who raised him from the dead and glorified him, and so your faith and hope are in God.
— *1 Peter 1:21 (NIV)*

If you confess with your mouth the Lord Jesus and believe in your heart that God has raised Him from the dead, you will be saved. For with the heart one believes unto righteousness, and with the mouth confession is made unto salvation.

—*Romans 10:9–10 (NKJV)*

And Jesus said to the woman, "Your faith has saved you; go in peace."

—*Luke 7:50 (NLT)*

Without faith, a person cannot please God. Any person who comes to God must believe that God is real. And any person who comes to God must believe that God rewards those people who truly want to find him.

—*Hebrews 11:6 (ERV)*

And so, dear brothers and sisters who belong to God and are partners with those called to heaven, think carefully about this Jesus whom we declare to be God's messenger and High Priest.
—*Hebrews 3:1 (NLT)*

Then Jesus told him, "Because you have seen me, you have believed; blessed are those who have not seen and yet have believed."
—*John 20:29 (NIV)*

Then Jesus answered and said to her, "O woman, great is your faith! Let it be to you as you desire." And her daughter was healed from that very hour.
—*Matthew 15:28 (NKJV)*

"Whoever comes to Me, and hears My sayings and does them, I will show you whom he is like: He is like a man building a house, who dug deep and laid the foundation on the rock. And when the flood arose, the stream beat vehemently against that house, and could not shake it, for it was founded on the rock. But he who heard and did nothing is like a man who built a house on the earth without a foundation, against which the stream beat vehemently; and immediately it fell. And the ruin of that house was great."

Now when He concluded all His sayings in the hearing of the people, He entered Capernaum. And a certain centurion's servant, who was dear to him, was sick and ready to die. So when he heard about Jesus, he sent elders of the Jews to Him, pleading with Him to come and heal his servant. And when they came to Jesus, they begged Him earnestly, saying that the one for whom He should do this was deserving, "for he loves our nation, and has built us a synagogue."

Then Jesus went with them. And when He was already not far from the house, the centurion sent friends to Him, saying to Him, "Lord, do not trouble Yourself, for I am not worthy that You should enter under my roof. Therefore I did not even think myself worthy to come to You. But say the word, and my servant will be healed. For I also am a man placed under authority, having soldiers under me. And I say to one, 'Go,' and he goes; and to another, 'Come,' and he comes; and to my servant, 'Do this,' and he does it."

When Jesus heard these things, He marveled at him, and turned around and said to the crowd that followed Him, "I say to you, I have not found such great faith, not even in Israel!" And those who were sent, returning to the house, found the servant well who had been sick.

—*Luke 6:47–7:10 (NKJV)*

Absolute DISCIPLESHIP

Then he called the crowd to him along with his disciples and said: "If anyone would come after me, he must deny himself and take up his cross and follow me. For whoever wants to save his life will lose it, but whoever loses his life for me and for the gospel will save it. What good is it for a man to gain the whole world, yet forfeit his soul? Or what can a man give in exchange for his soul? If anyone is ashamed of me and my words in this adulterous and sinful generation, the Son of Man will be ashamed of him when he comes in his Father's glory with the holy angels."
—*Mark 8:34–38 (NIV)*

But there in these other lands you will look for the Lord your God. And if you look for him with all your heart and soul, you will find him.
—*Deuteronomy 4:29 (ERV)*

Be proud of the Lord's holy name. All you people coming to the Lord, be happy! Look to the Lord and his strength. Always go to him for help.
—*1 Chronicles 16:10–11 (ERV)*

Imitate me, just as I also imitate Christ.
—*1 Corinthians 11:1 (NKJV)*

May the God who gives endurance and encouragement give you a spirit of unity among yourselves as you follow Christ Jesus.
—*Romans 15:5 (NIV)*

Anyone who wants to be my disciple must follow me, because my servants must be where I am. And the Father will honor anyone who serves me.
—John 12:26 (NLT)

And those who know Your name will put their trust in You; for You, LORD, have not forsaken those who seek You.
—Psalm 9:10 (NKJV)

You say that God is with you. So you should do good things, not evil. Then you will live. And the Lord God All-Powerful really will be with you.
—Amos 5:14 (ERV)

The LORD is good to those who depend on him, to those who search for him.
—Lamentations 3:25 (NLT)

One thing I ask of the LORD, this is what I seek: that I may dwell in the house of the LORD all the days of my life, to gaze upon the beauty of the LORD and to seek him in his temple.

—*Psalm 27:4 (NIV)*

You shall love the LORD your God with all your heart, with all your soul, and with all your strength.

—*Deuteronomy 6:5 (NKJV)*

And Stephen, full of faith and power, did great wonders and signs among the people. Then there arose some from what is called the Synagogue of the Freedmen (Cyrenians, Alexandrians, and those from Cilicia and Asia), disputing with Stephen. And they were not able to resist the wisdom and the Spirit by which he spoke. Then they secretly induced men to say, "We have heard him speak blasphemous words against Moses and God." And they stirred up the people, the elders, and the scribes; and they came upon him, seized him, and brought him to the council. They also set up false witnesses who said, "This man does not cease to speak blasphemous words against this holy place and the law; for

we have heard him say that this Jesus
of Nazareth will destroy this place
and change the customs which Moses
delivered to us." And all who sat in the
council, looking steadfastly at him, saw
his face as the face of an angel.

Then the high priest said, "Are these
things so?"

And he said, "Brethren and fathers,
listen: . . .

"Our fathers had the tabernacle
of witness in the wilderness, as He
appointed, instructing Moses to make
it according to the pattern that he had
seen . . .

"However, the Most High does not
dwell in temples made with hands, as
the prophet says: 'Heaven is My throne,
and earth is My footstool. What house
will you build for Me? says the LORD,
or what is the place of My rest? Has My
hand not made all these things?'

"You stiffnecked and uncircumcised in heart and ears! You always resist the Holy Spirit; as your fathers did, so do you. Which of the prophets did your fathers not persecute? And they killed those who foretold the coming of the Just One, of whom you now have become the betrayers and murderers, who have received the law by the direction of angels and have not kept it."

When they heard these things they were cut to the heart, and they gnashed at him with their teeth. But he, being full of the Holy Spirit, gazed into heaven and saw the glory of God, and Jesus standing at the right hand of God, and said, "Look! I see the heavens opened and the Son of Man standing at the right hand of God!"

Then they cried out with a loud voice, stopped their ears, and ran at him with one accord; and they cast him out of the city and stoned him. And the witnesses laid down their clothes at the feet of a young man named Saul. And they stoned Stephen as he was calling on God and saying, "Lord Jesus, receive my spirit." Then he knelt down and cried out with a loud voice, "Lord, do not charge them with this sin." And when he had said this, he fell asleep.

—*from Acts 6:8–7:60 (NKJV)*

 WITH JOY

I have rejoiced in your laws as much as in riches.
—*Psalm 119:14 (NLT)*

Lord, your Agreement is wonderful. That is why I follow it.
—*Psalm 119:129 (ERV)*

If they obey and serve Him, they shall spend their days in prosperity, and their years in pleasures.
—*Job 36:11 (NKJV)*

Remind the people to be subject to rulers and authorities, to be obedient, to be ready to do whatever is good.
—*Titus 3:1 (NIV)*

Help me understand, and I will obey
your teachings. I will obey them
completely.
　　　—*Psalm 119:34 (ERV)*

Those who obey God's commandments
remain in fellowship with him, and he
with them. And we know he lives in us
because the Spirit he gave us lives in
us.
　　　—*1 John 3:24 (NLT)*

I will walk about in freedom, for I have
sought out your precepts. I will speak of
your statutes before kings and will not
be put to shame, for I delight in your
commands because I love them. I lift up
my hands to your commands, which I
love, and I meditate on your decrees.
　　　—*Psalm 119:45–48 (NIV)*

If you love Me, keep My commandments.
   —*John 14:15 (NKJV)*

How do we know that we love God's children? We know because we love God and we obey his commands.
   —*1 John 5:2 (ERV)*

We know that we have come to know him if we obey his commands.
   —*1 John 2:3 (NIV)*

As obedient children, do not conform to the evil desires you had when you lived in ignorance. But just as he who called you is holy, so be holy in all you do.
   —*1 Peter 1:14–15 (NIV)*

CHARACTER PORTRAIT
MARY REJOICES IN *Obedience*

During Elizabeth's sixth month of pregnancy, God sent the angel Gabriel to a virgin girl that lived in Nazareth, a town in Galilee. The girl was engaged to marry a man named Joseph from the family of David. Her name was Mary. The angel came to her and said, "Greetings! The Lord (God) is with you. You are very special to him."

But Mary was very confused about what the angel said. Mary wondered, "What does this mean?"

The angel said to her, "Don't be afraid, Mary, because God is very pleased with you. Listen! You will become pregnant. You will give birth to a baby boy. And you will name him Jesus. He will be great (important). People will call him the Son of the Most High (God). The

Lord God will make him king like his ancestor David. Jesus will rule over the people of Jacob forever. Jesus' kingdom will never end."

Mary said to the angel, "How will this happen? I am still a virgin!"

The angel said to Mary, "The Holy Spirit will come to you and the power of the Most High (God) will cover you. The baby will be holy. He will be called the Son of God. Also, your relative Elizabeth is pregnant. She is very old, but she is going to have a son. Everyone thought she could not have a baby, but she has been pregnant now for six months! God can do anything!"

Mary said, "I am the servant girl of the Lord (God). Let this thing you have said happen to me!" Then the angel went away.

Mary got up and went quickly to a town in the hill country of Judea.

She went into Zechariah's house and greeted Elizabeth. When Elizabeth heard Mary's greeting, the unborn baby inside Elizabeth jumped. Then Elizabeth was filled with the Holy Spirit. Elizabeth said with a loud voice, "God has blessed you (Mary) more than any other woman. And God has blessed the baby which you will give birth to. You are the mother of my Lord, and you have come to me! Why has something so good happened to me? When I heard your voice, the baby inside me jumped with joy. What a blessing is yours because you believed what the Lord (God) said to you! You believed this would happen."

Then Mary said, "I praise the Lord (God) with all my heart. I am very happy because God is my Savior. I am not important. But God has shown his care for me, his servant girl. From now on, all people will say that I am blessed, because the Powerful One (God) has done great things for me. His name is very holy. God always gives mercy to those people that worship him. God reached out his arm and showed his power: He scattered those people that are proud and think great things about themselves. God brought down rulers from their thrones, and he raised up the humble people. God filled the hungry people with good things, but he sent the selfishly rich people away with nothing. God has helped Israel—the people he chose to serve him. He did not forget his promise to give us his mercy. God has done what he promised to our ancestors, to Abraham, and to his children forever."

—*Luke 1:26–55 (ERV)*

Learn TO RECOGNIZE GOD'S VOICE

I tell you the truth, anyone who sneaks over the wall of a sheepfold, rather than going through the gate, must surely be a thief and a robber! But the one who enters through the gate is the shepherd of the sheep. The gatekeeper opens the gate for him, and the sheep recognize his voice and come to him. He calls his own sheep by name and leads them out. After he has gathered his own flock, he walks ahead of them, and they follow him because they know his voice. They won't follow a stranger; they will run from him because they don't know his voice.

—*John 10:1–5 (NLT)*

Listen to counsel and receive instruction, that you may be wise in your latter days.

—*Proverbs 19:20 (NKJV)*

Listen to me, all who hope for deliverance—all who seek the LORD! Consider the rock from which you were cut, the quarry from which you were mined.

—*Isaiah 51:1 (NLT)*

This is how you can recognize the Spirit of God: Every spirit that acknowledges that Jesus Christ has come in the flesh is from God.

—*1 John 4:2 (NIV)*

In those days when you pray, I will listen.

—*Jeremiah 29:12 (NLT)*

Today I have given you the choice between life and death, between blessings and curses. Now I call on heaven and earth to witness the choice you make. Oh, that you would choose life, so that you and your descendants might live! You can make this choice by loving the LORD your God, obeying him, and committing yourself firmly to him. This is the key to your life. And if you love and obey the LORD, you will live long in the land the LORD swore to give your ancestors Abraham, Isaac, and Jacob.

—*Deuteronomy 30:19–20 (NLT)*

I will hear what God the LORD will speak, for He will speak peace to His people and to His saints; but let them not turn back to folly.

—*Psalm 85:8 (NKJV)*

Be still, and know that I am God; I will
be exalted among the nations, I will be
exalted in the earth.
      —*Psalm 46:10 (NIV)*

Listen to the LORD, you leaders of
"Sodom." Listen to the law of our God,
people of "Gomorrah."
      —*Isaiah 1:10 (NLT)*

Hear attentively the thunder of His
voice, and the rumbling that comes
from His mouth. He sends it forth
under the whole heaven, His lightning
to the ends of the earth. After it a
voice roars; He thunders with His
majestic voice, and He does not restrain
them when His voice is heard. God
thunders marvelously with His voice;
He does great things which we cannot
comprehend.
      —*Job 37:2–5 (NKJV)*

Lord, your teachings are good for me.
They are better than 1,000 pieces of
silver and gold.
　　　—Psalm 119:72 (ERV)

My sheep listen to my voice. I know
them, and they follow me.
　　　—John 10:27 (ERV)

CHARACTER PORTRAIT
YOUNG SAMUEL *Listens* TO GOD

Then the boy Samuel ministered to the LORD before Eli. And the word of the LORD was rare in those days; there was no widespread revelation. And it came to pass at that time, while Eli was lying down in his place, and when his eyes had begun to grow so dim that he could not see, and before the lamp of God went out in the tabernacle of the LORD where the ark of God was, and while Samuel was lying down, that the LORD called Samuel. And he answered, "Here I am!" So he ran to Eli and said, "Here I am, for you called me."

And he said, "I did not call; lie down again." And he went and lay down.

Then the LORD called yet again, "Samuel!"

So Samuel arose and went to Eli, and said, "Here I am, for you called me." He answered, "I did not call, my son; lie down again." (Now Samuel did not yet know the LORD, nor was the word of the LORD yet revealed to him.)

And the LORD called Samuel again the third time. So he arose and went to Eli, and said, "Here I am, for you did call me."

Then Eli perceived that the LORD had called the boy. Therefore Eli said to Samuel, "Go, lie down; and it shall be, if He calls you, that you must say, 'Speak, LORD, for Your servant hears.'" So Samuel went and lay down in his place.

Now the LORD came and stood and called as at other times, "Samuel! Samuel!"

And Samuel answered, "Speak, for Your servant hears."

—1 Samuel 3:1–10 (NKJV)

Believe IN THE POWER OF PRAYER

The LORD is far from the wicked, but He hears the prayer of the righteous.
—*Proverbs 15:29 (NKJV)*

You can pray for anything, and if you have faith, you will receive it.
—*Matthew 21:22 (NLT)*

I call on you, O God, for you will answer me; give ear to me and hear my prayer.
—*Psalm 17:6 (NIV)*

Blessed be God, Who has not turned away my prayer, nor His mercy from me!
—*Psalm 66:20 (NKJV)*

A person that hides his sins will not be successful. But a person that confesses his sins and stops doing wrong will receive mercy.
—*Proverbs 28:13 (ERV)*

But I, by your great mercy, will come into your house; in reverence will I bow down toward your holy temple.
—*Psalm 5:7 (NIV)*

Devote yourselves to prayer with an alert mind and a thankful heart.
—*Colossians 4:2 (NLT)*

Lord, your love is good. Answer me with all your love. With all your kindness, turn to me and help me!
—*Psalm 69:16 (ERV)*

The LORD has heard my supplication; the LORD will receive my prayer.
—*Psalm 6:9 (NKJV)*

Go back to Hezekiah, the leader of my people. Tell him, "This is what the LORD, the God of your ancestor David, says: I have heard your prayer and seen your tears. I will heal you, and three days from now you will get out of bed and go to the Temple of the LORD."

—*2 Kings 20:5 (NLT)*

Don't worry about anything; instead, pray about everything. Tell God what you need, and thank him for all he has done.

—*Philippians 4:6 (NLT)*

David built an altar to the LORD there and sacrificed burnt offerings and fellowship offerings. Then the LORD answered prayer in behalf of the land, and the plague on Israel was stopped.

—*2 Samuel 24:25 (NIV)*

Always tell each other the wrong things you have done. Then pray for each other. Do this so that God can heal you. When a good person prays hard, great things happen.

    —James 5:16 (ERV)

In every place of worship, I want men to pray with holy hands lifted up to God, free from anger and controversy.

    —1 Timothy 2:8 (NLT)

So we fasted and entreated our God for this, and He answered our prayer.

    —Ezra 8:23 (NKJV)

O LORD, hear my prayer, listen to my cry for mercy; in your faithfulness and righteousness come to my relief.

    —Psalm 143:1 (NIV)

Be joyful in hope, patient in affliction, faithful in prayer.

    —Romans 12:12 (NIV)

We cannot do things that are against the truth. We can only do things that are for the truth. We are happy to be weak, if you are strong. And we pray that you will grow stronger and stronger.

—*2 Corinthians 13:8–9 (ERV)*

Then the way you live will always honor and please the Lord, and your lives will produce every kind of good fruit. All the while, you will grow as you learn to know God better and better. We also pray that you will be strengthened with all his glorious power so you will have all the endurance and patience you need. May you be filled with joy, always thanking the Father. He has enabled you to share in the inheritance that belongs to his people, who live in the light.

—*Colossians 1:10–12 (NLT)*

The king wrote a special message. The king sent this message through the city: A command from the king and his great rulers: For a short time no man or animal should eat anything. No herd or flock will be allowed in the fields. Nothing living in Nineveh will eat or drink water. But every person and every animal must be covered with a special cloth to show he is sad. People must cry loudly to God. Every person must change his life and stop doing bad things. Then maybe God will change and not do the things he had planned. Maybe God will change and not be angry. Then maybe we will not be punished. God saw the things the people did. God saw that the people stopped doing evil things. So God changed and did not do what he planned. God did not punish the people.

—Jonah 3:7–10 (ERV)

LORD, I cry out to You; make haste
to me! Give ear to my voice when I
cry out to You. Let my prayer be set
before You as incense, the lifting up of
my hands as the evening sacrifice.
  —*Psalm 141:1–2 (NKJV)*

And this is my prayer: that your
love may abound more and more in
knowledge and depth of insight, so that
you may be able to discern what is best
and may be pure and blameless until
the day of Christ, filled with the fruit
of righteousness that comes through
Jesus Christ—to the glory and praise of
God.
  —*Philippians 1:9–11 (NIV)*

I pray that the faith you share will
make you understand every good thing
that we have in Christ.
  —*Philemon 1:6 (ERV)*

So when you pray, you should pray like this: "Our Father in heaven, we pray that your name will always be kept holy. We pray that your kingdom will come, and that the things you want will be done here on earth, the same as in heaven. Give us the food we need for each day. Forgive the sins we have done, the same as we have forgiven the people that did wrong to us. Don't let us be tempted (tested); but save us from the Evil One (the devil)."

—*Matthew 6:9–13 (ERV)*

CHARACTER PORTRAIT
Jesus' *Prayer*

Jesus spoke these words, lifted up His eyes to heaven, and said: "Father, the hour has come. Glorify Your Son, that Your Son also may glorify You, as You have given Him authority over all flesh, that He should give eternal life to as many as You have given Him. And this is eternal life, that they may know You, the only true God, and Jesus Christ whom You have sent. I have glorified You on the earth. I have finished the work which You have given Me to do. And now, O Father, glorify Me together with Yourself, with the glory which I had with You before the world was.

"I have manifested Your name to the men whom You have given Me out of the world. They were Yours, You gave them to Me, and they have kept Your word. Now they have known that all things which You have given Me are from You. For I have given to them the words which You have given Me; and they have received them, and have known surely that I came forth from You; and they have believed that You sent Me.

"I pray for them. I do not pray for the world but for those whom You have given Me, for they are Yours. And all Mine are Yours, and Yours are Mine, and I am glorified in them. Now I am no longer in the world, but these are in the world, and I come to You. Holy Father, keep through Your name those whom You have given Me, that they may be one as We are. While I was with them in the world, I kept them in Your name. Those whom You gave Me I have kept; and none of them is lost except the son of perdition, that the Scripture might be fulfilled. But now I come to You, and these things I speak in the world, that they may have My joy fulfilled in themselves. I have given them Your word; and the world has hated them because they are not of the world, just as I am not of the world. I do not pray that You should take them out of the world, but that You should keep them from the evil one. They are not of the world, just as I am not of the world. Sanctify them by Your truth. Your word is truth. As You sent Me into the world, I also have sent them into the world. And for their sakes I sanctify Myself, that they also may be sanctified by the truth.

"I do not pray for these alone, but also for those who will believe in Me through their word; that they all may be one, as You, Father, are in Me, and I in You;

that they also may be one in Us, that the world may believe that You sent Me. And the glory which You gave Me I have given them, that they may be one just as We are one: I in them, and You in Me; that they may be made perfect in one, and that the world may know that You have sent Me, and have loved them as You have loved Me."

—*John 17:1–23 (NKJV)*